OUR FAMILY
Prays

CATHOLIC PRAYERS
& TRADITIONS

PETER M. ESPOSITO
President

ANNE P. BATTES
Publisher

JO ROTUNNO
Publisher Emerita

MARY SELLARS MALLOY
Project Editor

CREDITS AND ACKNOWLEDGMENTS

NIHIL OBSTAT
IMPRIMATUR
† Most Reverend Joseph R. Binzer
Auxiliary Bishop; Vicar General
Archdiocese of Cincinnati
Cincinnati, Ohio
June 22, 2015

The *Nihil Obstat* and *Imprimatur* are official declarations that the material reviewed is free of doctrinal or moral error. No implication is contained therein that those granting the *Nihil Obstat* and *Imprimatur* agree with the contents, opinions, or statements expressed.

Multicultural Specialist:
    Francisco Castillo, DMin
Design: Mary Wessel

Send all inquiries to:
RCL Benziger
8805 Governor's Hill Drive, Suite 400
Cincinnati, Ohio 45249

Toll Free 877-275-4725
Fax 800-688-8356
Visit us at **RCLBenziger.com**

20863
ISBN: 978-0-7829-0417-8
Our Family Prays
Catholic Prayers & Traditions
1st Printing June 2015

ACKNOWLEDGMENTS
Mardi Gras contributor: Ken Richard.

Excerpts are taken or adapted from *Catholic Household Blessings and Prayers* (revised edition) © 2007, United States Conference of Catholic Bishops, Washington, D.C. All rights reserved.

The Book of Blessings *(Copyright © 1989, The Order of St. Benedict, Inc.) offers the Order for the Blessing of Seeds at Planting Time (see* Book of Blessings *986-1006), pp. 27-29.*

PHOTO AND ILLUSTRATION CREDITS
Cover, © Michael O'Neill McGrath, OSFS © Bee Still Studio, beestillstudio.com, 410.398.3057; Inside Cover, © Labetskiy Alexandr/Shutterstock; p4 © Michael O'Neill McGrath, OSFS © Bee Still Studio, beestillstudio.com, 410.398.3057; p6 © Michael O'Neill McGrath, OSFS © Bee Still Studio, beestillstudio.com, 410.398.3057; p7 © mythja/iStock/Thinkstock, © Photodisc/Thinkstock; p8 ©mythja/iStock/Thinkstock, © mart_m/iStock/Thinkstock; p9 © Dudarev Mikhail/Shutterstock; p10 ©mythja/iStock/Thinkstock, © Dan Rossini/iStock/Thinkstock, © Bill Wittman; p11 © Belinka/iStock/Thinkstock; p12 © Kari Marttili/Alamy, © Diana Taliun/iStock/Thinkstock; p13 ©ArtParts, © clipartdotcom/iStock/Thinkstock; p14 © ArtParts, © Tinica/iStock/Thinkstock, ©olomc-ottawa.com; p15 © rionm/iStock/Thinkstock, © Gabhor Utomo, Represented by StoryBook Arts, Inc.; p16 ©Route55/iStock/Thinkstock, ©Mervana/iStock/Thinkstock; p17 © ArtParts, ©LiliGraphie/iStock/Thinkstock; p18 © rionm/iStock/Thinkstock, © RCL Benziger, ©tibori/iStock/Thinkstock; p19 ©Thinkstock, © Mario Ragma/Hemera/Thinkstock; p20 © ArtParts, © Tinica/iStock/Thinkstock, ©Rosemary Buffoni/iStock/Thinkstock; p21 © Thinkstock, ©RCL Benziger; p22 © clip art library; p23 © ArtParts; p24 ©Tinica/iStock/Thinkstock, © Michael O'Neill McGrath, OSFS © Bee Still Studio, beestillstudio.com, 410.398.3057, © Bill Wittman; p25 © rionm/iStock/Thinkstock, ©1971yes/iStock/Thinkstock; p26 © Tinica/iStock/Thinkstock, © Jupiterimages/liquidlibrary/Thinkstock, © Bill Wittman; p27 © rionm/iStock/Thinkstock, © Will Heap/Thinkstock, © feellife/iStock/Thinkstock; p28 © sofiaworld/iStock/Thinkstock; p29 © Dynamic Graphics/liquidlibrary/Thinkstock, ©Yarruta/iStock/Thinkstock; p30 © malija/iStock/Thinkstock, © Véronique Lestoquoy/iStock/Thinkstock, © Aspire Images; p31 © AspireImages, © AspireImages, © Design Pics/Ron Nickel/Getty; p32 © Ewa Mazur/iStock/Thinkstock, © Nelosa/iStock/Thinkstock; p33 © Jose Elias/iStock/Thinkstock; p34 © ArtParts, © Teneresa/iStock/ Thinkstock, © Ecelop/iStock/Thinkstock, © jozef sedmak/iStock/Thinkstock; p35 ©rionm/iStock/Thinkstock, © Banana Stock/Thinkstock; p36 © Tinica/iStock/Thinkstock, © nikolaj2k/iStock/Thinkstock, © Fuse/Thinkstock; p37 © ArtParts, ©Tinica/iStock/Thinkstock, © Marmaduke St. John / Alamy; p38 © ArtParts, © salemcatholic.org; p39 © ArtParts, © James Shaffer / PhotoEdit, © Tinica/iStock/Thinkstock; p40 © Jack Hollingsworth/Digital Vision/Thinkstock, © Design Pics/Leah Warkentin/Thinkstock, © Chad Baker/Photodisc/Thinkstock; p41 © rionm/iStock/Thinkstock, © Jupiter; p42 ©rionm/iStock/Thinkstock; p43 © amana imagesRF/Getty; p44 © rionm/iStock/Thinkstock, ©3DMaster/iStock/ Thinkstock, © tassel78/iStock/Thinkstock, © Bill Wittman, © Visual Source Photography, © Bill Wittman, © lrochka_T/iStock/Thinkstock, © Anton Balazh/iStock/Thinkstock; p45 © 3DMaster/iStock/Thinkstock; p46 © rionm/iStock/Thinkstock; p47 © Vjom/iStock/ Thinkstock; p48 ©bestdesigns/iStock/Thinkstock; Inside Bk Cov © Labetskiy Alexandr/Shutterstock; Bk Cov © Michael O'Neill McGrath, OSFS ©Bee Still Studio, beestillstudio.com, 410.398.3057, © Labetskiy Alexandr/Shutterstock.

TABLE OF CONTENTS

Dedication 4

Using this Resource 5

Liturgical Year Calendar 6

ADVENT 7

Prayer for the New Church Year 8

Blessing of the Advent Wreath 10

Around the World: Las Posadas 13

Around the World: Novena to the Divine Child ... 14

CHRISTMAS 15

Blessing of the Christmas Tree 16

Around the World: The Unexpected Guest 17

Blessing of the Home on Epiphany 18

LENT 19

Around the World: Mardi Gras & King Cake 20

Take Up Your Cross 21

Around the World: Global Awareness 23

With My Family: Palm Sunday 24

EASTER 25

With My Family: Easter Sunday Light of Christ 26

The Blessing of Seeds 27

Adorning an Image of the
Blessed Virgin Mary 30

Mysteries of the Rosary 33

Around the World: Pentecost 34

ORDINARY TIME 35

With My Family: Summertime Lantern Walk 36

Around the World: Quinceañera 37

Around the World: Saint Anthony's Bread 38

Around the World: Dia de los Muertos 39

With My Family: Solemnities and Feasts
in Ordinary Time 40

BLESSINGS AND PRAYERS FOR EVERYDAY LIFE 41

For Families 42

For the Celebration of the Sacraments 44

For Life's Occasions 46

DEDICATION

RCL Benziger dedicates Our Family Prays *to your family and all families! We believe that your family is a gift from God and we are thankful for the opportunity to walk this faith journey with you.* Our Family Prays *is devoted to help strengthen family living through the power of prayer.*

Beginning with the season of Advent, we invite you and your family to journey through the liturgical life of the Church. Experience the prayers of our Church and blessing prayers for everyday family life. Live the diverse and rich traditions of families and the Church from different cultures throughout the world. Foster a life of prayer to strengthen and empower each family member to live as a disciple of Jesus Christ.

Let the Holy Spirit guide us all into a lifetime of prayer allowing God to fill our hearts with his everlasting love. **From our family to yours, may the blessings of the Holy Family give you strength and hope as we journey together with Our Family Prays.**

USING THIS RESOURCE

This book includes seasonal rituals, blessings, shorter prayers, and devotions and practices that connect us to the universal Church. They are organized according to the liturgical seasons of the Church year, beginning with the season of Advent.

Begin by signing and dating the book. Choose the seasonal prayers and suggestions that will best engage all members of your household. If a ritual or blessing is too lengthy for your younger children, choose the parts of the ritual that will work for you. Likewise, think of creative ways to expand upon the shorter devotions and blessings in order to further enrich your family's celebration of them.

It is our prayer that this resource will inspire you to fulfill Saint Paul's encouragement to rejoice always and to pray without ceasing (see 1 Thessalonians 5:16,17).

THE NEW CHURCH YEAR

The new Church year, also called the liturgical year, begins on the First Sunday of Advent. And so it seems fitting that this family prayer and ritual book begins with a prayer for the new Church year.

Before celebrating A Prayer for the New Church Year, take time to download a larger version of the calendar on the next page, or create or purchase a liturgical year calendar of your choosing. Decide where you will display your calendar.

Color in the seasons all at once, or as they unfold: purple for Advent and Lent; white or gold for Christmas, the Easter Triduum, and Easter; and green for Ordinary Time. Put special stickers or stars on the calendar as you celebrate the holy days of obligation, and other feasts and solemnities honoring Jesus, Mary, and the Saints.

Items needed for A Prayer for the New Church Year are: a Bible; your liturgical year calendar; and a way to display the calendar. Invite family members to serve as the leader of prayer, the Scripture reader, and the reader of A Litany of Time.

Now, turn to page 8 and celebrate as a family A Prayer for the New Church Year!

THE Liturgical YEAR CALENDAR

Advent

Christmas

Ordinary Time

Lent

Easter

Ordinary Time

Easter Triduum

Download a reproducible liturgical year calendar at

RCLBLectionary.com

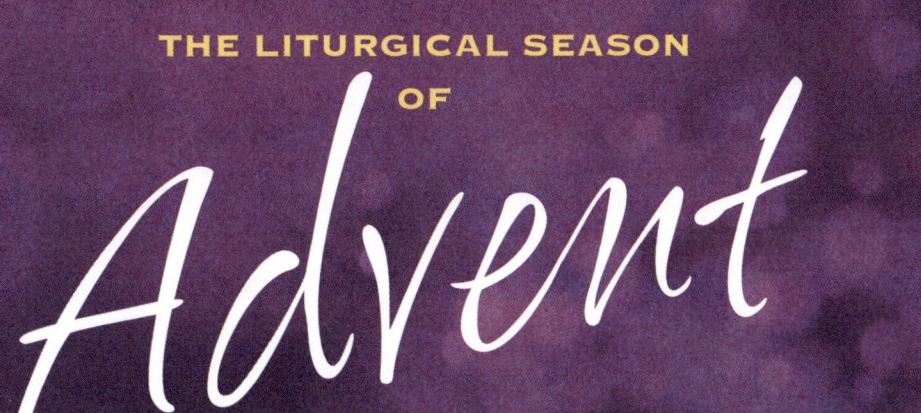

THE LITURGICAL SEASON
OF
Advent

JESUS,
YOU ARE OUR LIGHT.

WHEN YOU CAME INTO OUR WORLD,
YOU MADE IT A BRIGHTER PLACE.

HELP US EACH DAY TO MAKE
BRIGHTER AND HAPPIER
THE LIVES OF THE PEOPLE WE LIVE WITH,
LEARN WITH, PLAY WITH, AND PRAY WITH.

AMEN.

Prayer FOR THE New Church Year

INTRODUCTORY RITES

Gathering Song: *Sing the refrain of "Soon and Very Soon" or another familiar Advent hymn or refrain.*

Sign of the Cross: *Pray together the Sign of the Cross.*

Leader: Let us pray.

God of all time,
today we begin a new Church year.

Help our family to celebrate it well
in our prayer and in our living.

We ask this through Christ our Lord.
Amen.

THE WORD OF GOD

Scripture Reading: *Genesis 1:14-18 or Ecclesiastes 3:1-11*

Leader: Invite family members to share their favorite time of the day, of the year, and of the Church year.

A LITANY OF TIME

Reader: **Our time is in your hands.**

1. As we celebrate the new Church year,
   with its seasons and feasts,
   help us remember –

2. As we watch the news and hear about
   what is happening in the world,
   help us remember -

3. As we think about our lives,
   our family, and our future,
   help us remember -

4. When we get up in the morning
   and go into the day,
   help us remember -

5. When day comes to an end
   and night time comes,
   help us remember -

6. When we look at the sun, the moon,
   and the stars in the sky,
   help us remember -

7. When we put on a watch, look at at clock,
   or check to see what time it is,
   help us remember -

POSTING THE NEW CHURCH YEAR CALENDAR

Invite a family member to hang the new Church year calendar.

Leader: God of all time,
may this calendar remind us
that every day and every season
are created by you.

As we celebrate the new Church year,
open our minds and our hearts
to learn more about you,
and about Jesus, Mary, and all the Saints
who walked in your way.

We ask this through Christ our Lord.
Amen.

CONCLUDING RITES

Sign of the Cross: *Pray together the Sign of the Cross.*

Concluding Song: *Conclude by again singing the Gathering Song.*

ADVENT + ADVENT + ADVENT + ADVENT + ADVENT

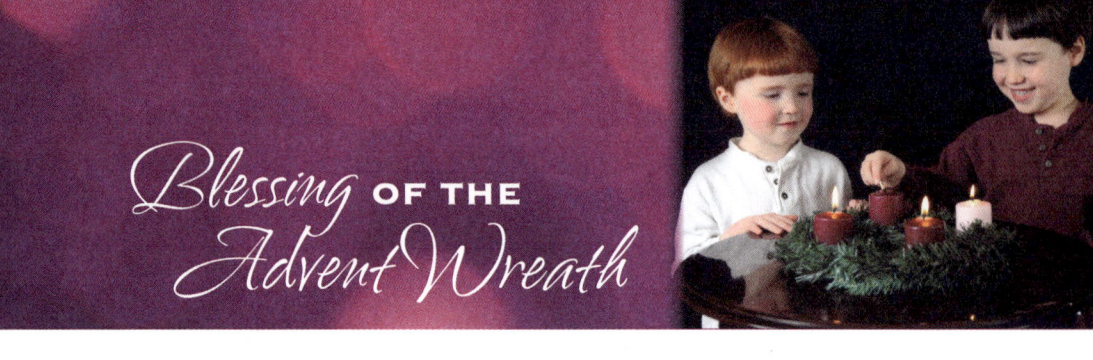

Blessing OF THE *Advent Wreath*

INTRODUCTION

The Advent wreath is a popular custom that is celebrated in churches and homes all over the world. Its origins go back to pagan times. Its Christian symbolism was introduced in Germany in the 1600s. The wreath is made of a circle of evergreens in which are placed three purple candles and one pink (rose) candle.

The circular shape of the wreath reminds us that the love of God is without beginning or end. The evergreens represent the hope of everlasting, or eternal, happiness. The candles remind us that Jesus, the Light of the world, came to Earth to overcome the darkness of sin and selfishness. The purple candles represent our need to prepare for the coming of the Savior, and the pink (rose) candle—lit on the Third Sunday of Advent— reminds us to be joyful, for the coming of the Lord is near!

Celebrate this Blessing of the Advent Wreath with your family. You will need the wreath and candles, matches or a lighter, and a Bible. Invite family members to serve as the leader of prayer, the reader of Scripture, and the reader of the intercessions.

INTRODUCTORY RITES

Gathering Song: Begin by singing together a familiar Advent hymn or refrain.

Sign of the Cross: Pray together the Sign of the Cross.

ADVENT ✦ ADVENT ✦ ADVENT ✦ ADVENT ✦ ADVENT

Leader: In many parts of the world, when the season of winter comes, the darkness of night is longer, and people wait for the daylight of spring. In the Church, when Advent comes, Christians wait for the coming of Jesus, the Light of the world. Let us open our ears and our hearts today to hear God's Word about light.

WORD OF GOD

Scripture Reading: *Isaiah 9: 1-2, 5-6 or 1 John 1: 5-7*

Reflection:
1. Invite family members to name things that give light.
2. Next, invite everyone to name ways that people give light.
3. Finally, invite each person to quietly think of one way they can share the light of Jesus with another person in the week to come.

INTERCESSIONS

Reader: **Come, Lord Jesus.**

1. For the Church, working to share your Good News with all, we pray –
2. For the world, especially places longing for peace, we pray –
3. For the hungry, the homeless, and all in need, we pray –
4. For the sick, and for all who care for them, we pray –
5. For our family, as we begin our celebration of Advent, we pray –

BLESSING OF THE ADVENT WREATH

Leader: Loving God,
your Son, Jesus Christ,
is the Light of the world.

Bless our family as we light this wreath
and enter into the season of Advent.

May its candles remind us to share Christ's light
through our words and deeds.

Amen.

(Light the first candle of the Advent wreath.)

CONCLUDING RITES

Blessing: *Make the sign of the cross as you say the following:*

Now may Jesus, the Light of the world,
guide our words and actions
and fill our hearts with peace.
Amen.

Concluding Song: *Conclude by singing an Advent hymn or refrain.*

Continue to light the Advent wreath throughout the season of Advent. Use the Blessing Prayer (above) as your wreath-lighting prayer, modifying the fifth line of the prayer to read "and celebrate the season of Advent." The Intercessions and concluding Blessing are also appropriate for the entire season of Advent.

Las Posadas

A TRADITION FROM MEXICO

One Advent tradition from Mexico is Las Posadas – "the inns." This tradition involves a community procession from house to house. Neighbors play the parts of Mary and Joseph and other characters of the Christmas story, and walk through the town carrying candles and singing carols. At each home, the Holy Family looks for lodging but is told, "There is no room in the inn." Finally, at the last house, the couple is let in. Prayers, singing, rejoicing, and feasting follow.

Here are three suggestions for celebrating Las Posadas with your family.

1 Lead the family from room to room as you look for a place for Jesus to be born. At the doorway of each room, knock and ask if there is room. Invite a family member to respond, "No, no! There is no room here." End the search in the dining room or kitchen. Ask if there is room, and have a family member again respond, "No, no! There is no room here." Then ask, "Then where is there room?" Invite the whole family to reply, "There is always room in our hearts!" End the journey with laughter, hugs, and a tasty treat.

2 Extend the celebration to include your neighbors. As a family, go from door to door to tell your neighbors how happy you are to be members of the neighborhood. You could even dress up like the Holy Family. Take a small treat to each family you visit.

3 Pick an Advent evening to go as a family to a few of your nearby neighbors. Invite them to come over to your house for coffee and hot chocolate and dessert. Be spontaneous! Don't be hurt if nobody comes. You are letting your neighbors know, "There is room in our inn!"

Novena to the Divine Child

A TRADITION FROM LATIN AMERICA

Every year families and communities throughout Latin America and other parts of the world celebrate nine days of prayer to the Child Jesus called the Novena to the Divine Child. A *novena*, nine days of prayer, often leads up to the celebration of a major feast or solemnity of the Church, such as Christmas, Easter, or Pentecost Sunday.

The Novena to the Divine Child begins on December 16. People gather to pray, sing hymns, share meals, and even dance. At the start of the novena, Christmas trees are decorated and the Nativity set is already set up. But the celebrations stop at midnight on Christmas Eve so that the presents, which the Child Jesus has brought for the children, can be opened.

WITH MY FAMILY

Host your own celebration of the Novena to the Divine Child. Starting on December 16, gather as a family and invite friends and neighbors to your home to pray. Research the Internet for resources for prayer or write your own prayers. Prepare some food to share, and choose some Advent and Christmas music to sing at your gatherings.

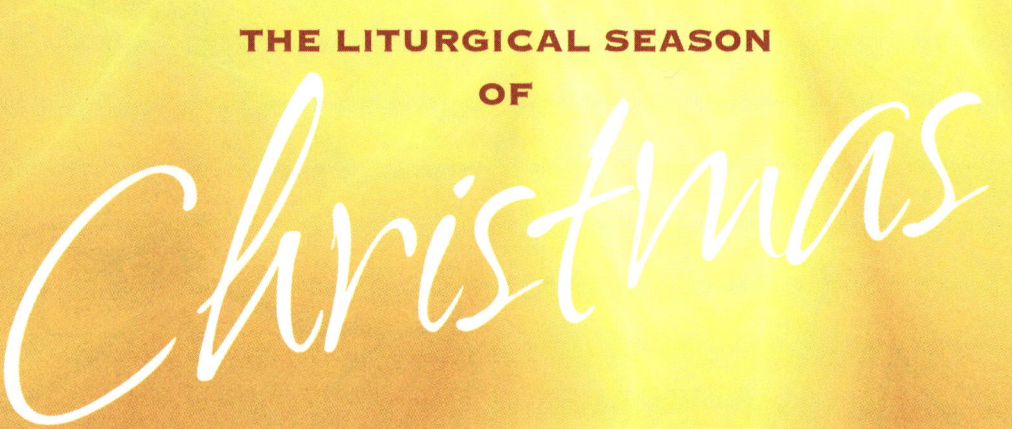

THE LITURGICAL SEASON
OF
Christmas

O GOD,
DURING THE CHRISTMAS SEASON
WE ARE FILLED WITH
THE LIGHT OF YOUR LOVE.

WITH THE COMING OF YOUR SON, JESUS,
MAY THE LIGHT OF FAITH SHINE
IN OUR WORDS AND ACTIONS.

AMEN.

CHRISTMAS ✦ CHRISTMAS ✦ CHRISTMAS ✦ CHRISTMAS

Blessing OF THE Christmas Tree

INTRODUCTION

Before celebrating this blessing, you will need to invite one family member to be prepared to light the tree, and another family member to be prepared to place a new or special ornament upon the tree.

Begin by inviting family members to gather around the unlit Christmas tree.

Sing together a verse of a favorite Christmas carol, pray together the Sign of the Cross, and then offer the following prayer of blessing:

**God of all creation,
as we gather around this tree,
we ask your blessing upon us.**

(The appointed family member should light the tree.)

**May your light surround us,
and show us the way to love and serve you
throughout this Christmas season.**

(The appointed family member should place the ornament upon the tree.)

**May all who gather here with us
enjoy the beauty of this tree,
the warmth of laughter,
and the gift of friendship.**

**We ask this through
Christ our Lord.
AMEN.**

CHRISTMAS ✦ CHRISTMAS ✦ CHRISTMAS ✦ CHRISTMAS

The Unexpected Guest

A TRADITION FROM CHINA, CZECHOSLOVAKIA, AND POLAND

In many countries such as China, Czech Republic, Slovakia, and Poland, it is the tradition to leave one extra place setting at the Christmas Eve dinner table for an unexpected guest. This is to celebrate the tradition of welcome and hospitality. The empty seat is for a family member, friend, or stranger who may come seeking food and warmth. In some traditions, the unexpected guest is Jesus, and the place is set as a sign that he is welcome in the family's home and at the family's table.

As you set your Christmas table, set an extra place, and pray for all of those who are in need of warmth, food, welcome, and hospitality. Pray that your family may always welcome the Christ in them with kindness and generosity.

The Christmas Créche

A TRADITION FROM ITALY

Saint Francis of Assisi staged the first live Nativity scene in a cave near the village of Grecio (in Italy) in the year 1223. He created the scene for villagers to come and enjoy as he preached the Good News of the birth of the Savior. The custom of displaying Nativity sets in our homes has its origins in this event.

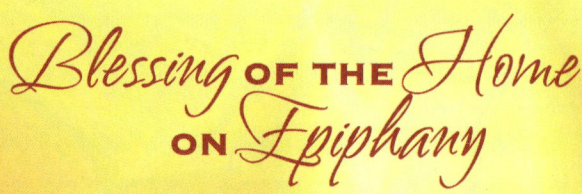

Blessing OF THE Home ON Epiphany

In many places it is custom to celebrate the blessing of the home by writing the numerals of the new year in chalk over the front door, as well as the initials C, M, and B—representing the traditional names of the Magi—Caspar, Melchior, and Balthasar. This would look like the following: 20 + C + M + B + 15.

Gather the family outside the front door or main entrance of your home. Begin by singing "We Three Kings" and by praying together the Sign of the Cross. Then offer the following prayer of blessing:

**Loving God,
the doors of our hearts and the doors of our home
are open to you and
to all who need warmth and welcome.**

*(Write the year and the initials C, M, and B in chalk over
the front door or main entrance of your home.)*

**We give you thanks for our home,
for the gift of family, and for the blessing of friends.**

**Keep us safe
as we come in and as we go out
each and every day.**

We ask this through Christ our Lord.

Amen.

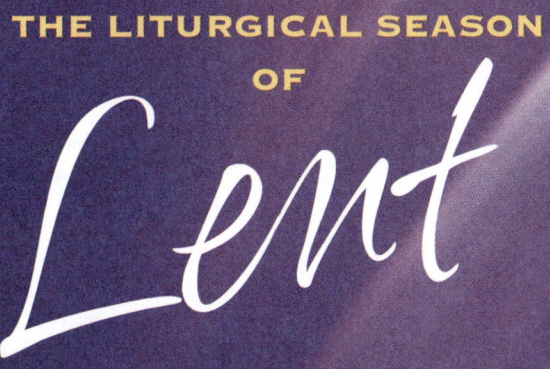

THE LITURGICAL SEASON
OF
Lent

OUR SIGN IS THE CROSS.

AND SO WE PRAY:

IN THE NAME OF THE FATHER,

AND OF THE SON,

AND OF THE HOLY SPIRIT.

AMEN.

LENT ✦ LENT ✦ LENT ✦ LENT ✦ LENT ✦ LENT ✦ LENT

Mardi Gras
AND KING CAKE

King Cake is part of the celebration of Epiphany and Carnival. The word *Carnival* means "farewell to flesh" and refers to the Lenten fast and abstinence. This is also the time when families eat the King Cake (the *Galette des Rois*), whose round and twisted shape represents the winding route the Magi took to hide the location of baby Jesus from Herod. Whoever finds the image of baby Jesus that is hidden in the cake is crowned the "king" of the party, and is expected to host the next King Cake party.

WITH MY FAMILY

In the days before Lent begins, celebrate the Epiphany and Carnival with a King Cake! Search the Internet for King Cake recipes and ideas. Gather the family to share the King Cake, offering the following prayer:

Lord, as we gather to enjoy this King Cake, we remember the joy of your Epiphany. May this cake's sweetness sustain us during the time of Lenten fasting. May its shape remind us of the journey the Magi made to pay you homage. May its colors lead us to seek justice, to live lives of faith, and to recognize your power and majesty. Amen.

INTRODUCTION

In preparation for the prayer, invite one family member to serve as the leader of prayer, one to serve as the reader of Scripture, and one to serve as the reader of the intercessions.

As a family, take a walk through your yard or through your neighborhood, and invite each family member to find two small twigs or pieces of wood. Have them tie these together with string or yarn to form a simple cross.

Gather your family around the kitchen table or around your family prayer table, and invite each person to place his or her cross on the table.

Begin prayer by singing a Lenten gathering song or refrain, and then pray together the Sign of the Cross.

Continue the prayer as follows:

Leader: During Lent we walk with Jesus. We hope to share in the Resurrection of Easter. God's Word guides us on our journey.

Scripture Reading: *Mark 10: 35-45*

Leader: Jesus looked ahead to the cross he would bear. Are you willing to take up your crosses this Lent?

All: **WE ARE!**

Leader: Let us pause and take time to consider one thing we know we need to do to be more like Jesus. *(Pause for silent reflection. Then, ask each family member the following question.)*

(Name), will you take up your Lenten cross and follow Jesus?

Response: I will!

(Invite each family member to take a wooden cross from the prayer table. It does not need to be the cross that he or she made.)

Conclude the prayer as follows.

Leader: Our response is, "Lord, help us follow you."

Reader: As we take up our Lenten crosses and begin our Lenten journey, we pray —

All: **LORD, HELP US FOLLOW YOU.**

Reader: As we walk with each other, answering your call to love God and neighbor, we pray —

All: **LORD, HELP US FOLLOW YOU.**

Reader: Here at home, at school, at church, and when with friends, we pray —

All: **LORD, HELP US FOLLOW YOU.**

Reader: As we walk in faith toward the joy of Easter, we pray —

All: **LORD, HELP US FOLLOW YOU.**

Leader: Loving God,
you alone are our source of strength
and faith.

Help us support one another as we
take up our crosses, signs of our
love for Jesus, who carried his Cross
because of his great love for each of us.

We ask this through Christ our Lord.

All: **AMEN.**

Conclude this prayer by singing a Lenten hymn or refrain focusing on the Cross and/or on following Jesus.

Global Awareness

WORLD HUNGER

As part of your family's Lenten fasting, consider eating simple meals and donating the money you would normally spend on a family dinner to your CRS rice bowl, to your parish food pantry, or to a local food bank.

The following are three suggestions to help raise your family's awareness of those throughout the world and in your own community who do not have enough food to eat.

1 Almost two-thirds of the world lives on a diet composed mostly of rice and beans. One Lenten evening, have a meal consisting of only these two items. Talk about what family members know about people around the world. Talk about the need for peace and justice for people of all races, colors, and beliefs. End the meal with a prayer for freedom from poverty, hunger, war, and oppression around the world and in your own community.

2 Have a similar meal on another Lenten evening. Again prepare some of the staples of the Third World—rice, beans, pita, or tortillas, and the like. During the course of this meal, talk about places in the world where there is suffering. You may want to share a couple of articles from the newspaper or from your diocesan paper or parish bulletin. When the meal is finished, again pray for those who suffer from hunger, poverty, war, and oppression of any kind.

3 On a third Lenten evening, set pictures of the poor and oppressed on your dining table. Again serve the staples of the Third World. Talk about people in the world who hunger and places in the world where there is suffering. At the end of the meal, pray for all the people and places you have mentioned. As a family, decide on one practical way you can help the poor and hungry in your community and/or in the world.

Palm Sunday

In Jesus' time, people sometimes used objects as they prayed. Palm branches were used during prayers of praise. The waving branches symbolized victory. Jesus' followers held palm branches during his triumphant entry into Jerusalem before his Passion and Death.

Palms are blessed at the beginning of the Palm Sunday liturgy. The ashes crossed on our forehead on Ash Wednesday come from burned palms. Some families place palms around a hanging crucifix or a holy picture. Another tradition is braiding palms into crosses. As a family, search the Internet for directions for making simple palm crosses.

THE NUMBER FORTY

Noah's forty days and nights on the ark, the Israelites' forty years of wandering in the wilderness, Jesus' forty days in the desert, the forty days of Lent: all highlight the number forty. In ancient times, the number forty symbolized a long period of time or a period of testing, waiting, and change.

As a family, search the Internet to find other Scriptures that highlight the number forty.

THE LITURGICAL SEASON
OF
Easter

Alleluia!

Jesus,
you made us your special friends
through the waters of Baptism.

Help us to treat others as friends.

Amen. Alleluia!

EASTER ✦ EASTER ✦ EASTER ✦ EASTER ✦ EASTER

Easter Sunday

LIGHT OF CHRIST

Work together to create an Easter candle for your home. Get a large white candle, and use stickers, permanent markers, glitter paint, and other available arts and crafts supplies and natural materials to decorate the candle with the name of each family member and symbols of Easter and new life. Keep the candle on display from Easter Sunday through Pentecost Sunday. It will remind you that the Light of Christ will never go out in your home! Light the candle during family meals or during family prayer times. Add to your prayer times an Easter proclamation such as, "Christ is risen! Alleluia! He is truly risen! Alleluia!" OR a sung Alleluia or Easter refrain.

Alleluia!

THE PASCHAL (EASTER) CANDLE

As a family, take a closer look at the symbols on the Paschal (Easter) candle at church, the candle blessed and lit from the Easter Vigil fire. It represents Christ, the Light of the world. Look for the symbols for Alpha (A) and Omega (Ω), the current year, and the cross (representing Christ).

See if five grains of incense have been inserted into the candle in the form of a cross. These represent the five wounds of Christ: his hands; his feet; and his side.

THE *Blessing* OF *Seeds*

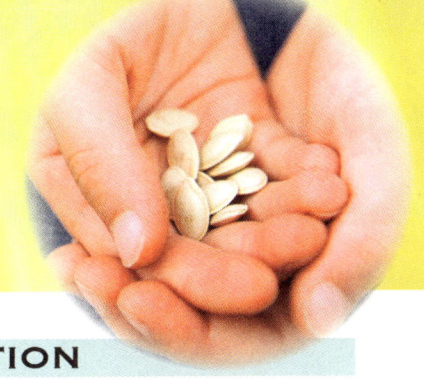

INTRODUCTION

Preparing to Pray

Arrange the seeds or seedlings on a table, along with some of the hand tools needed for planting (trowel, garden gloves, watering can, etc.).

Invite family members to serve as the leader of prayer, the reader of Scripture, and the reader of the prayer of the faithful.

THE BLESSING

Introductory Rites

Sing a hymn or refrain about creation, or a festive Alleluia.

Pray together the Sign of the Cross.

Words of introduction

Leader: Today we will ask God's blessing on the seeds (the seedlings) here on our table, knowing that the plants they will produce will bring beauty to the earth and food to our table.

Let's listen to a Scripture story about seeds and growing.

EASTER + EASTER + EASTER + EASTER + EASTER

THE WORD OF GOD

Gospel Acclamation: *Sing an Alleluia known by all family members.*

Scripture Reading: *Matthew 13:31-32 or Mark 4:26-29*

Leader: *Discuss what kinds of seeds your family plants by your words and actions each day (seeds of kindness, joy, hope, love, faith, etc.).*

Then invite each family member to come forward and choose a packet of seeds (or seedling). Invite them to hold their seeds or seedling as the prayer continues.

PRAYER OF THE FAITHFUL

Leader: God provides the seeds, and sends the rain and the sun to help them grow. Let us turn to God in prayer.

Reader: For the Church.

May she continue to plant the seeds of faith and justice in the world today.

We pray to the Lord.

All: **LORD, HEAR OUR PRAYER.**

Reader: For those in need.

May the seeds of our money, time, and love help those who are hungry, those in need of shelter and clothing, and all in need of special care.

We pray to the Lord.

All: **LORD, HEAR OUR PRAYER.**

Reader: For the farmers.

May the seeds they plant this spring grow and produce much food.

We pray to the Lord.

All: **LORD, HEAR OUR PRAYER.**

Reader: For the prayers of our hearts.

(Pause for a moment of quiet reflection, or invite family members to share their prayers.)

We pray to the Lord.

All: **LORD, HEAR OUR PRAYER.**

PRAYER OF BLESSING AND CONCLUSION

Leader: *Invite family members to hold high their seeds or seedlings as you offer the following prayer.*

God our Creator,
you have given us many gifts of creation
and you have asked us
to care for them all.

We ask your blessing
as we go forth to plant these
seeds (seedlings).

As we care for them,
help us remember to also
care for those in need
so that your love and goodness
may grow in our hearts
and in the hearts of all we meet.

We ask this through Christ our Lord.
AMEN.

Conclude by singing a refrain or song celebrating God's gifts of creation, and by planting your seeds and seedlings!

Adorning AN IMAGE OF THE *Blessed Virgin Mary*

May is traditionally a month in which Catholics honor Mary by praying the rosary, celebrating May Crowning, or gathering for prayer in her honor. This prayer is appropriate for the month of May, or for any feast or solemnity of the Church year on which Mary is honored.

Create a Marian devotional area on your family prayer table or in a special place in your home. You will need:

- A statue, picture, or image of the Blessed Virgin Mary or multiple images of Mary representing many cultures
- Candles
- Fresh flowers
- A basket of rosaries (one for each family member)

Invite family members to serve as the leader of prayer and as the reader of Scripture.

INTRODUCTORY RITES

Gather the family around the prayer table or designated devotional area. Invite family members to hold the image(s) of Mary, candles, flowers, and basket of rosaries until it is time to place them on the prayer table.

Gathering Song: Begin by singing a familiar refrain or song in honor of Mary.

Sign of the Cross: Pray together the Sign of the Cross.

Introduction:

Leader: Catholics honor Mary as Christ's mother, as the Mother of the Church, and as the Church's greatest Saint.

(Invite family members to share other things they know about Mary.)

May is a special month in the Church to honor Mary.

Let us open our hearts to hear Mary's words of joy and praise taken from the Gospel of Luke.

THE WORD OF GOD

Gospel Acclamation: *Sing a Gospel Acclamation (Alleluia) familiar to your family.*

Gospel Reading: *Luke 1: 42-50*

Leader: *Invite family members to share why Mary rejoiced in God, and the things that cause them to rejoice in God, too.*

LITANY OF MARY

(Based upon the Litany of Loreto)

Lead the speaking, chanting, or singing of the following litany.

Leader	All
Holy Mary	pray for us
Mother of God's Son	pray for us
Mother of the Church	pray for us
Model of holiness	pray for us
Model of patience	pray for us
Model of motherhood	pray for us
Queen of families	pray for us
Queen of all saints	pray for us
Queen of the rosary	pray for us
Cause of our joy	pray for us
Morning Star	pray for us
Help of Christians	pray for us
Queen of peace	pray for us

EASTER • EASTER • EASTER • EASTER • EASTER

ADORNING THE PRAYER TABLE OR DEVOTIONAL AREA

Sing a Marian song or hymn as the prayer table or devotional area is adorned with the image(s) of Mary, the candles, the flowers, and the basket of rosaries.

PRAYER OF BLESSING AND CONCLUSION

Leader: Loving God,
may our family,
gathered here to honor Mary,
learn the way of holiness
through the example of her life,
and grow in faith and love.

We ask this through Christ our Lord.

All: AMEN.

Leader: Let us pray together:

All: HAIL, MARY. . .

Continue to gather for prayer at the prayer table or devotional area throughout the month of May.

Mysteries

As your family gathers to pray the Rosary in May and throughout the year, invite family members to read the short Scripture passages connected with each mystery of the Rosary.

Joyful Mysteries
1. The Annunciation (Luke 1:28)
2. The Visitation (Luke 1:41-42)
3. The Nativity (Luke 2:7)
4. The Presentation in the Temple (Luke 2:22-23)
5. The Finding of the Child Jesus After Three Days in the Temple (Luke 2:46)

Luminous Mysteries
1. The Baptism at the Jordan (Matthew 3:16-17)
2. The Miracle at Cana (John 2:5-7)
3. The Proclamation of the Kingdom and the Call to Conversion (Matthew 10:7-8)
4. The Transfiguration (Luke 9:29,39)
5. The Institution of the Eucharist (Matthew 26:26-28)

Sorrowful Mysteries
1. The Agony in the Garden (Luke 22:43-44)
2. The Scourging at the Pillar (Mark 15:15)
3. The Crowning With Thorns (Matthew 27:28-29)
4. The Carrying of the Cross (Matthew 27:31-32)
5. The Crucifixion and Death (John 19:28,30)

Glorious Mysteries
1. The Resurrection (Mark 16:6)
2. The Ascension (Mark 16:19)
3. The Descent of the Holy Spirit at Pentecost (Acts 2:4)
4. The Assumption of Mary (Revelation 12:1)
5. The Crowning of the Blessed Virgin as Queen of Heaven and Earth (Revelation 12:1)

Pentecost
CELEBRATIONS

The celebration of Pentecost Sunday differs around the world. In Italy, it was long ago customary to throw rose leaves from church ceilings to symbolize the fiery tongues. In France, trumpets were blown to recall the sound of the mighty wind that came with the descent of the Holy Spirit. In Russia, people carry flowers and green branches in a procession. Pilgrims journey to an annual Pentecost festival held in El Rocio in southern Spain.

As a family, decide on one or more ways to celebrate Pentecost Sunday. Wear red, the liturgical color of Pentecost Sunday. Bake and enjoy a special cake to celebrate the birthday of the Church! Make and wave streamers of red, orange, and yellow to symbolize the tongues of fire. Fly a kite, and think of the mighty wind of the Spirit blowing throughout the earth. Learn and say together the Prayer to the Holy Spirit:

Come, Holy Spirit, fill the hearts of your faithful.

And kindle in them the fire of your love.

Send forth your Spirit and they shall be created.

And you will renew the face of the earth.

THE LITURGICAL SEASON

OF

Ordinary
TIME

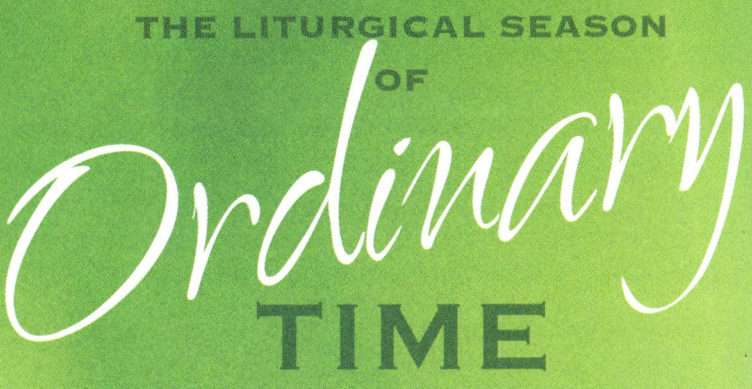

DEAR GOD,
THE WARMTH OF THE SUN
ON OUR FACES FEELS GOOD.

THE LIGHT OF THIS DAY SHINES ON IN US.

YOUR BRIGHT LOVE, O GOD,
ALSO SHINES EVERYWHERE.
IT SHINES ON OUR WORK AND OUR PLAY.

KEEP US ALWAYS
IN THE WARM LIGHT OF YOUR LOVE.
AMEN.

ORDINARY TIME • ORDINARY TIME • ORDINARY TIME

Summertime Lantern Walk

Processions are traditional prayers of movement. Catholics process as they pray the Stations of the Cross, on festival days, and during Las Posadas. If you have a big enough yard, hold a summertime procession with your family and friends. Carry lanterns, votive candles, or even flashlights, and march around the yard. Stop four or five times, and at each stop, say, "In the light of these lanterns (these candles/ these flashlights) we pray for the needs of . . ." Invite all in the procession to name their prayers for the families represented, for the neighborhood, for the country, and for the world. After offering prayers at the final stop, conclude by praying together the Lord's Prayer. You may wish to sing a song about light (such as "This Little Light of Mine" or "Christ Be Our Light") as you process from stop to stop.

Autumn Altar

Set aside a place in the home for an autumn altar. Place upon your altar a cloth in a fall shade of green, the family Bible, a candle, and then take a family walk. Invite each family member to find one or two items of nature to place upon the autumn altar. This altar will be a sign for your family that Jesus is present in your home all fall. Gather at this altar for morning prayer or night prayer throughout the week.

Quinceañera

A TRADITION FROM LATIN AMERICA

Quinceañara is a tradition of mainly Spanish-speaking countries that is celebrated when a young girl turns fifteen. Some consider it to be a rite of passage from childhood to maturity. The celebration encompasses religious customs, family traditions, and social responsibility. It most often begins with a religious ceremony, followed by a reception including a choreographed dance performed by the young girl and her court, and a toast to offer congratulations.

WITH MY FAMILY

Gather where the celebration will take place. Invite a parent, grandparent, or godparent to read a favorite Scripture passage. Conclude by offering the following prayer.

Lord, fifteen years ago you gave our family a daughter. She is a wonderful blessing, filling our days with love and joy. We give thanks for the honor of being a part of her life. Today we again present her to you. May she continue to praise you always with her beauty and her smile. May her tears be an offering for peace and justice in the world. May she always seek you in your Word and in the Sacraments. Amen.

Saint Anthony's Bread

A TRADITION FROM ITALY

Many people think of Saint Anthony's Bread as a charitable donation of food or money. These are given to the Church, especially to Franciscan friars, on behalf of the poor and in thanks for prayers answered through the intercession of Saint Anthony of Padua.

One legend connected to this tradition dates back to 1263, to the story of a child who drowned near the Basilica of Saint Anthony in Padua. The child's mother made a promise to distribute food to the poor if Saint Anthony returned her child alive. The miracle was granted, and she fulfilled her promise.

Some parishes and individual members of the Franciscan order distribute loaves of bread on June 13, the Feast of Saint Anthony of Padua. On this day, the priest also blesses baskets of bread for people to take home and enjoy at dinnertime.

WITH MY FAMILY

On or near June 13, take the family to buy food to donate to your parish food pantry or to a local food bank. Before delivering your gifts for the poor, pray:

Lord of all goodness, you fasted and hungered in the desert, and you broke and blessed the bread that continues to nourish us today.

Following the example of Saint Anthony of Padua, who cared for the poor and hungry, bless these gifts of food that we will share with those in our community who do not have enough food to eat.

Amen.

Día de los Muertos

DAY OF THE DEAD

Since *Día de Los Muertos* (Day of the Dead) falls on the first days of November, people often confuse it with Halloween. However, Halloween is filled with spirits and demons who terrorize the living one night of the year. The Day of the Dead, a popular celebration in Mexico, grows from the beliefs of native peoples who thought of death as part of the life cycle.

The Catholic Church in Mexico has moved the holiday to coincide with All Saints on November 1, dedicating that day to the children who have died. November 2, All Souls' Day, is dedicated to the adults who have died. These are days for festivity, not somberness, and they include costumes, special foods, celebrations at church, and gatherings at cemeteries.

WITH MY FAMILY

Create a family altar for *Día de Los Muertos* (Day of the Dead). Select a few pictures of family members and friends who have died, and images of special Saints and the Virgin Mary. Place these on the altar, adding candles, flowers, and the traditional skull- and skeleton-shaped candies. Gather at the altar and invite family members to offer memories of and prayers for the deceased.

Solemnities and Feasts
IN ORDINARY TIME

In addition to the Solemnities of the Assumption of the Blessed Virgin Mary (August 15) and All Saints (November 1), the Church celebrates many other wonderful solemnities and feasts during the liturgical season of Ordinary Time.

As a family, research the history of one or more of the following solemnities and feasts, and celebrate these days by attending Mass or by singing a special song of praise and celebration as you gather for family prayer time.

The Presentation of the Lord
February 2

The Nativity of John the Baptist
June 24

The Transfiguration of the Lord
August 6

The Nativity of the Blessed Virgin Mary
September 8

The Exaltation of the Holy Cross
September 14

Saints Michael, Gabriel, and Raphael, Archangels
September 29

The Holy Guardian Angels
October 2

All Souls' Day
November 2

BLESSINGS AND PRAYERS FOR

Everyday LIFE

BLESSINGS AND PRAYERS FOR FAMILIES

BLESSINGS AND PRAYERS FOR THE
CELEBRATION OF THE SACRAMENTS

BLESSINGS AND PRAYERS FOR LIFE'S OCCASIONS

BLESSINGS AND PRAYERS FOR EVERYDAY LIFE

Blessings AND PRAYERS FOR Families

Prayer for Welcoming Home a Newborn or Adopted Child

God of all life,
today our hearts are filled with joy
as we welcome home

_____ (name).

May this be the first of many days
of joy, blessing, laughter, and love.

May our home be a place

where _____ (name)
learns what it means to be family–
trusting, forgiving, sharing, loving,
and growing as your children
in faith, hope, and love.

Amen.

Blessing of Children

As your child leaves for school or sports, a class trip or the events of the day, take a moment to sign his or her forehead with the sign of the cross. As you do so, pray one of the following blessing prayers or a blessing prayer in your own words.

May God bless you today. Amen.

May God keep you safe today.
Amen.

Today may you know my/our love
and God's love, too. Amen.

May you be blessed with friendship,
joy, and love today. Amen.

Prayer for Mothers

Dear Jesus,
you loved your mother, Mary,
very much.

Bless my mother.
Help her with the work
she has to do today.

Help me to show her
love and respect
in all I say and do.

Amen.

Prayer for Fathers

Dear Jesus,
you loved and obeyed Joseph,
your father on Earth.

Bless my father.
Help him with the work
he has to do today.

Help me to show him
love and respect
in all I say and do.

Amen.

Prayer for a Family

Dear Jesus,
your Holy Family is
the model for all families.

Mary was a loving mother,
Joseph was a caring father,
and you were their holy child.

Our family is different from yours,
but we want to grow in holiness,
goodness, and love.

Help us to care for each other
as Mary, Joseph, and you
cared for each other.

Help us to show our love for you
by loving and serving each other
in what we say and in what we do.

With your help,
may our family be known as a
holy family, too.

Amen.

Blessing of Grandparents

Lord God almighty,
bless our grandparents with
long life, happiness, and
health.
May they remain constant in
your love
and be living signs of your
presence
to their children and
grandchildren.
We ask this through
Christ our Lord.

Amen.

Blessing for a Pet

O God,
you ask us to care for and
to enjoy the creatures
of the earth.

Bless our pet, _____ (name).
Keep him/her safe and healthy.
Help us to care for him/her.

Amen.

BLESSINGS AND PRAYERS FOR FAMILIES

Blessing Before Celebrating the Sacrament of Baptism

God of new life,
today we celebrate the
Baptism of

_____ (name).

As _____ (name)
begins her/his journey as your
beloved daughter/son,
may she/he always know
your love and the love
of this family, too.

Amen.

Blessing Before Celebrating First Penance and Reconciliation

God of Mercy,
today our child

_____ (name)

celebrates his/her First Penance
and Reconciliation.

May _____ (name)
always know that, no matter what,
you are a loving
and forgiving God.

May our family show

_____ (name)
your mercy and love
by the way we love
and forgive each other.

Amen.

Blessing Before Celebrating First Eucharist

Jesus, Bread of Life, today we celebrate First Eucharist with

_____ (name).

As _____ (name)
shares in your holy banquet,
may she/he taste your goodness
and know your presence
in her/his life.

May the Eucharist strengthen

_____ (name)
to honor your
Great Commandment to
love and serve God
and neighbor
now and always.

Amen.

Blessing Before Celebrating Confirmation

Spirit of Life,
today we celebrate the
Confirmation of

_____ (name).

Fill _____ (name)
with your Gifts that he/she
may remain strong in faith
and use his/her talents
to serve God and others.

Amen.

Blessing Before Celebrating Marriage

*In some countries, it is customary
to give a blessing to the daughter
or son who is about to marry.
This blessing is often offered by
the parents or grandparents as
their son or daughter prepares
to leave home to go to the church
for the celebration of the
Sacrament of Marriage. The son
or daughter kneels and asks for
the blessing from his or her
parents or grandparents.*

God of love,
today our son/our daughter,

_____ (name),

and _____ (name)
will celebrate the
Sacrament of Marriage.

Bless them as they
enter into this covenant of love.

May this day
and the days to come
be days of rejoicing and blessing

for _____ (name)

and _____ (name).

May they grow to be
a sign of your love,
known for their kindness,
generosity, and hospitality.

Amen.

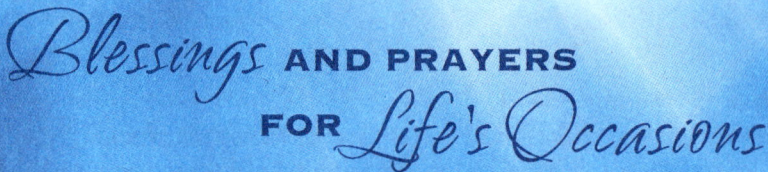

Blessings AND PRAYERS FOR Life's Occasions

Blessing for Life's Special Occasions

Every stage of life presents its unique moments that invite us to turn to God in prayers of celebration, blessing, and praise. A young child celebrates the first day of school, riding the bus for the first time, his or her first report card. A teen takes part in a sporting event, receives his or her own set of car keys, attends his or her first dance, prepares to leave home for college, and starts his or her first full-time job. An adult receives a promotion, a new job, is transferred to another city or country, travels abroad, and retires.

The following prayer is a suggestion for use when celebrating each of these special moments and more.

God our Creator,

today we ask your special blessing

upon _____ (name),

who is celebrating

_____ (occasion).

We rejoice in this good news

in his/her life.

We ask you to bless,

protect, and guide _____ (name)

now and always.

Amen.

Blessing on Birthdays

Loving God,
you created all the people
    of the world,
and you know each of us
    by name.
We thank you for _____,
    (pray the person's name)
who celebrates his/her birthday.

Bless him/her with your love
    and friendship
that he/she may grow in
    wisdom, knowledge, and grace.
May he/she love his/her
    family always
and be ever faithful to his/her
    friends.
Grant this through Christ
    our Lord.

Amen.

Prayer for Each New Day

God of all time,
as we leave our home
to go to school and work today,
we ask your blessing.

Help us give our studies and
our work our best efforts.
Show us ways to help
our classmates and coworkers.
Make us mindful of your presence
in every minute and every hour.

And bring us safely home,
that we may share
the stories of the day
and the warmth of your love.

Amen.

Blessing on Anniversaries

God of love,

as _____ (name)

and

_____ (name)
today celebrate their anniversary,
renew, bless, and strengthen
their covenant of love.

Fill their hearts with joy,
and help them continue to be
a sign of your love among us,
welcoming, encouraging,
comforting, and helping
family members, friends,
and all they meet.

Amen.

Prayer for an Empty Nest

Mother Mary,
today the house seems so quiet,
and I am feeling so alone.

Memories of a house full of children,
laughter, and love,
are haunting me.

I am missing those times.

Give me the grace
to sit in the silence,
to let the tears fall,
and then to find joy in the memories.

Give me the grace
to continue the work of this day,
knowing that I am never alone.

Amen.

BLESSINGS AND PRAYERS FOR LIFE'S OCCASIONS

Prayer During Sickness

As you pray the following prayer, make the sign of the cross on the forehead of the person you are praying for by name.

Jesus, Healer,
we pray in a special way for

_____ (name) today.

Comfort _____ (name),
and all who are sick
and in need of healing,
with your love.

Amen.

Prayer at the Death of a Loved One

God of eternal life,
today the Saints and angels welcomed

_____

(name) home to Heaven.

But our hearts are sad at the loss of our family member (our friend).

Help us in our sadness,
and give us strength to help each other in the days to come.

Amen.